In my youth I soon set off in search of the meaning of life. But they said that life has its origins in some primordial alchemy of Nature! This appalled me and only strengthened my resolve to look closely into Origins and Evolution, yet staying forever true to my heart – for the mystery of life is infinitely greater than Nature herself; and the mystery of love belongs to eternity.

After many years, God, who created the Universe, revealed Himself to me, and all the pieces of the puzzle one by one fell into place. At last, Science had found its origins and humankind had found our home.

ORIGINS, EVOLUTION,
AND THE COVENANT OF LOVE

ORIGINS, EVOLUTION, AND THE COVENANT OF LOVE

Written by <u>Simon Lars,</u>
servant of GOD.

Vanguard Press

VANGUARD PAPERBACK

© Copyright 2014
Simon Lars

The right of Simon Lars to be identified as author of
this work has been asserted by him in accordance with the
Copyright, Designs and Patents Act 1988.

A CIP catalogue record for this title is
available from the British Library.

ISBN – 978-1-84386-983 2

*Vanguard Press is an imprint of
Pegasus Elliot Mackenzie Publishers Ltd.*
www.pegasuspublishers.com

First Published in 2014

**Vanguard Press
Sheraton House Castle Park
Cambridge England**

Printed & Bound in Great Britain

Contents

Prelude to the book

"So, from that First Moment that Our God BEGAN the work of Creation (ref. Genesis 1:1–2), I shall believe that Creation itself became the Object of His Love, and thus, Love and Wisdom and Might were engaged upon Creation...yet with perfect foresight and knowledge He 'foresaw' ultimately the creation of MAN.

Indeed, God would not have begun His Work without having in mind the creation of MAN -male and female- from the start.

Let it be said, however, that God did not bring into being the wonder of Life on Earth in six days literally but over millions of years; nor that living things were fashioned by chance but in fact by design, according to His pre-ordained purposes."(quoted from 'The Holy Covenant of Love', Chapter 2) ... which now continues:

"God's creative hand used every facet of the material and living world to move Creation onward and upward, allowing natural agents and processes to assist Him while He exercised order and absolute control over everything, miraculously (and genetically) bringing into being new species according to their timely purpose(s), and ultimately arriving at the wondrous and diverse world we know today.

Be it said also, that nothing was created yet now extinct which did not have a significant part to play in bringing about the fulfilment of His Plan. So when we read that 'others have done the hard work and we have reaped the benefits of their labours,' (John 4:38), **I think it is right for us not to forget from whence we came, notwithstanding the fact that we are body, soul and spirit, for otherwise we are not truly Human at all!"**

In my first work, entitled, *'The Holy Covenant of Love'* (Vanguard Press 2014), I testify to the true meaning and nobility of Humanity made by the Creator to rejoice in His Blessed Company and Love. Within no time at all of completing this, I was again urged by God to compile another book, *'Origins, Evolution, and the Covenant of Love'* which enlightens us to our Past and that of all Creation, so that we may understand better our physical biological roots and our spiritual God-centred roots. One might say then, that having revealed the Portrait of True Humanity in book one, book two sets this into the context of the greater Picture according to God's immutable purpose for Creation which still awaits The Fulfilment.

PREFACE

It is my belief that only when we arrive at a true synthesis of Science and Religion will we be enabled to uncover the mystery of life on earth and of our own true origins. For too long now, this has been the preserve of Science without the 'light' of Divine Revelation to give understanding and meaning. On the opposite side stands Religion, with no apparent need for the empirical evidence of Science. Indeed, there is little or no dialogue between these two, yet, just as we all agree that Religion with no regard for Science is 'fundamentalism', so too is the same true for Science. This book, therefore, seeks a proper synthesis between the two, compatible and sharing a common vision.

Such reconciliation is long overdue, for it is no longer tenable for us to stick with the belief that Evolution is grounded in mere chance and random events giving rise to such inexplicable and fortuitous change that we find ourselves here today! Science declares that 'evolution' is an unending chain-reaction based upon a set criteria of biological and environmental factors, yet seemingly without any ultimate meaning or purpose. It is precisely here that Religion can fill this vacuum and give answer to our deepest questions about existence.

So if we profess to be seeking the truth, then we must take the bull by the horns and deal with the consequences... if we believe that TRUTH is on our side. I cannot speak for others, but as a 'Believer' I must gaze in wonder at the fossil record and at the archaeological findings, and with my hands full of questions take these before God. Indeed, having been *called* to carry out this work, I have done precisely this and God has provided the answer which I now share with you.

It is my hope that you will see conclusively that rather than a self-governing process of 'natural selection' on the back of incredulous and chance mutations, what Palaeontology and Archaeology uncovers for us is in fact the trace-line of **Intelligence at work** upon life in a material world, and that this world has been brought into being for <u>a most noble purpose</u> which has yet to be fulfilled.

It was my hope to include the expertise of the Scientific Community into this work to ensure that the data I use is accurate, but alas, just as I have made no friends amongst the Religious Community on account of my first book,* so in like manner, the Scientific Community no doubt prefers to turn a blind eye to this book too! (see Appendix)

Lucky for me then that today I can speak openly for all to hear just as God intends me to do. You may laugh and that's OK for I have not left a sense of humour behind in my work, so you may yet enjoy another chuckle or two. Nevertheless, my intention here is to open our minds and hearts to the message of Love and of Life Itself.

*The Holy Covenant of Love:
Testimony to our True Humanity
Vanguard Press, 2014

PART ONE

THE TRUE MEANING OF 'EVOLUTION'

INTRODUCTION

Ever since the 'Big Bang' brought the material world into existence; ever since an enormous rock crashed into the molten earth, sending vast quantities of material into space, held in orbit by gravity and resulting in the accretion of a moon, itself essential for the origin and development of life on earth, stabilising the motion of the earth and creating the tides; ever since comet-water rained down upon the hot primordial earth, which itself had just been knitted together so wonderfully by Gravity; ever since those green primordial Stromatolite-fields which decked the shallow sea-beds, feeding off all that nasty carbon dioxide that filled the air, and giving off all that life-giving oxygen through photosynthesis, (oxygen which more complex creatures would depend on); ever since the earth's primeval atmosphere was first primed with enough oxygen to sustain an ozone layer to protect the terrestrial earth from those nasty radiation-rays of the sun: ever since all these things happened, we have seen the wonders of timely 'coincidences'! The earth orbiting its Sun at just the right distance away so as to receive just the right warmth and light, together with the 'waters in the heavens' (Genesis 1:6–7) sent down right at the start to bless the earth with the medium of life. In all this, can we seriously think it is all by chance?!

Of course, we can never be so sure that these events happened as recounted here, but we know for certain that timely causes brought about propitious effects which, put all together, resulted in extraordinarily successful enterprise! From where I am looking, this cannot be by chance!

So what I hope to show is that there is indeed much to wonder about, how a Creator-God is in fact responsible for doing it all for His own good purpose, indeed, so that ultimately we mere creatures would live in blissful harmony and union with Him who created us. This is after all the crux of the Christian message.

Indeed, if the scientist was to allow himself for a moment to make his judgements upon this understanding which gives the process of evolution **meaning and purpose**, then he would recognise that <u>Intelligence</u> is behind every trace of every process of every happening through the passage of 'evolutionary' time. And that all of this vast journey we call 'evolution' is but the necessary means to an ultimate end, according to the will of Him who determined it in the first place. (ref. Genesis 1:1)

This story, therefore, is grounded in both religion and science, a proper synthesis complimenting each other's understanding of existence. It's only when we do this that we can build a true Picture, preserving the serious matter of our need for meaning, purpose and design, not to mention the sublime rhythms and details of Beauty that imbues so much of the natural world.

So let us allow God to show us the way, and how science should follow His lead, so that we may explore the material world as an encounter of Divine Providence. Indeed, it is by looking at the world of today as the planned outcome of the whole story of evolution that we will most readily put the pieces of this evolutionary-puzzle together, and since we were the last of God's work which completed the Picture resulting in the Garden being blessed with God's own Very Presence, (ref. Genesis 3:8), we may see everything that came before this moment as the Work towards this goal, when ultimately, "God saw all that He had made, and it was not just good but **VERY** good". (Genesis 1:31)

Nevertheless, we know from Scripture that this perfect outcome was subjected to frustration on account of Man's disobedience, for Man did not conform to God's Will when he was tested in the Garden of Eden. (Genesis 2:16) And so, for this reason, the whole Creation must wait until God's final Intervention for which our Humanity yearns, for <u>we are incomplete as we are</u> and must awaken to Life-in-God as was always meant for us if we are to assume our rightful place in the wondrous World to come.

So I invite you to sit with me as I recount a small part of this immense story, and even if you are forced to chuckle to yourselves at my audacity, perhaps sound reasoning will win the day after all! For the Story told is nearing its end... when Creation shall arrive at **'The Fulfilment'**, according to God's pre-ordained Plan.

EVOLUTION BY DESIGN

Of course, having made my case so boldly, I had better do so convincingly! So, in what wise can I possibly prove my case?

Let me explain:

When two important factors are found to be vital contributors to the development of something new, which in turn are proved to play a vital role in creating a new environment without which new species could not exist, then we might think that this was a fortuitous coincidence. If there were three such factors, we might think the same, but not if there were ten! If all ten worked in perfect unison seemingly fated to do this wonderful task, then I think we would agree that there must be Intelligent Intervention at work, One who is making it all happen to bring about a pre-ordained outcome.

However, one might say that the whole of 'evolution' is an ongoing string of interconnected factors bringing about new conditions and new outcomes, but since everything takes place in such an enormous time-scale it is bound to be difficult to prove the presence of God's pre-eminent and active role.

But let us see, let us look at the finer details to prove my case (on God's behalf) which I think will capture the hearts and minds of those of us who are reasonable, and since 'ten factors' goes to prove it, I will come up with **ten**... a compilation of key factors coming together at one time to bring about a single and life-changing outcome, in that each factor played its essential part for that outcome.

Thus, I am going to tell the story about the Dinosaurs, how it is that they were the <u>indispensable</u> player in this saga of life on earth as we know it.

"So what on earth did the dinosaurs do for us?" I hear you say...

What I wish to impress upon the reader is my belief that the Dinosaurs were invaluable in preparing the way from out of a primordial world and into the world not so dissimilar from today. In fact, one might say that it was on the back of the 'work' given them by God that served to create the necessary platform for modern life by which we find ourselves here today!

Where would we be without the birds to grace our sky, and there is every reason to believe that they have their origins from the dinosaurs. The mystery of feather and flight is extraordinary and beyond us to comprehend since the miraculous is so evident, but my little story about 'Bronto' (if you will excuse this 'generic' label given for Dinosaurs, especially the giant herbivorous **Sauropods**) is more down to earth and much easier for us to understand, so that's where we must go.

Thus, this story tells us much about the mastery of THE CREATOR working out every facet of the material world, including climate and environment, all in order to bring about His ultimate Plan for the living World. It is my hope that this re-telling will enlighten us to our proper place in the grand scheme of things. For ever since our 'fall from grace' so very long ago (see Genesis 3:11) our relationship with and perception of life is not as it ought to be, characterised by a prevalent 'lonely' self-centredness. The fact is that we were never meant for such a self-styled existence without our Master by our side! For just as the animals instinctively live in step with a Providential God who tends to their needs, no less so were we meant to enjoy the guardianship and intimate company of our Creator through an interpersonal Covenant of Love. Therefore, when we turn the pages of evolutionary time, let us do so with this in mind, notwithstanding the ultimate goal for Creation for which sacrifice would have to be made along the way, (ref. John 4:38) and for which **The Sacrifice** would have to be made at its conclusion. (ref. John 19:30)

So we can be sure that whatever the Dinosaurs did for us was done well. However, if Bronto had followed our manner of self-interested determination, then the outcome would have been self-destructive. But since he must conform instinctively within the balance that holds everything in order, he is sure to do **good** work, pleasing to God. Just imagine if he had done things as farmers are prone to do, of maximising productivity and yield! Imagine if he were to overpopulate, out-graze and up-raze everything around him! All too much and too quick to do a proper job as he was told to do! Yet despite the heavy burden of his size, he dominated the flat expanse of the earth over a vast time-scale... all in order to get a good job done. He did not know it, but his Master did, and that's all that matters. Such is the stuff of Nature under the Mighty Hand of God, fulfilling its task and bringing Him glory as She does.

THE BRIDGE THAT WAS
BUILT BY 'BRONTO'

What I need to make clear is that my hypothesis stands not so much on evidence *per se* but upon the intended and resulting outcomes. In other words, everything is by design. For I declare that nothing that happened or was created during this great saga of evolution was by chance, but that all things were brought into being for some good purpose. And so we have in the story of 'Bronto' the Dinosaurs who built *the bridge* over which complex life would travel, and once accomplished, we know that God sent another vast rock from space to do His bidding at the Great Extinction of 65 million years ago. Let me explain with the use of a metaphor:

Imagine if you will, that you and your Family were stranded in a land which did not fit your aspirations in any way, but that you knew of a land just over the River that was like a dream come true. Alas, there was no way of getting across that River! Only by building a bridge could you get you and your Family across to lay hold of the destiny that awaited in a new Land where your Family would truly thrive and find happiness.

The environment of the super-continent Pangaea fitted the needs of the Dinosaurs and evergreen Gymnosperms perfectly:

this was the '**Primordial World**'. But such a place was completely incompatible for more complex 'modern' life. Everything had to change! Pangaea had to break up, mountains and valleys had to be built, rivers and seas had to be formed, and above all, a top-soil had to be made, all the necessary environmental conditions suitable to support the arrival and expansion of a new order of life – the complex and sexual Mammals, Birds, and fruit-bearing insect-pollinating Flowering Plants: this I call the '**New World**', the world that God intended from the start. And it is clear from the fossil record that the juncture between the 'Primordial' and 'New' began during the age of the dinosaurs and came to an explosive transformation with their extinction some 65 million years ago. Not a single Dinosaur made it into the New World, whereas the sexual complex world of life flourished in an unprecedented way! The 'bridge', however, does not refer to 65, but in fact to the outcome of the 'Big Ten'. What happened at 65 we may say shut the door on the 'Primordial World' forever, because now, the blessed Land awaited the immense diversity of complex life that was latent and waiting to bloom. And I hope to show by the 'Ten' how we have the Dinosaurs to thank for that!

Yes, Bronto did his ground-work very well, and lived to see out 135 million years, but God for-saw the New World to come, which of necessity meant the demise of the Old. By now Pangaea was long gone, and the continents were blessed with mountains and rivers and valleys and plains. Rather than the flat monotype warm stable environment of Pangaea, we now have seasonal variation and geographical variety opening the door to a wide range of plants and animals finding a wide range of new environments to enjoy and make their home in, living an interconnected life-style far more complex than the 'Primordial World' of old. Indeed, one might say that intelligent and truly sexual life was set free to 'evolve' and thrive as never before... just as God intended.

DINOSAUR:
A means to an end

Preamble

The Dinosaurs first appeared in Late Triassic when reptiles, the first truly terrestrial animals, and conifers, the first seed-bearing forests, dominated the earth. By the Jurassic period the Dinosaurs dominated the scene. Everything submitted to their presence and seemed well capable of supporting such enormous beasts that ranged over the vast, flat and monotone environment of Pangaea before the land was divided up and drifted apart upon those mighty and shifting 'plates tectonic', to form a variety of continents and taking with them a wide diversity of herbivorous, omnivorous, and carnivorous Dinosaurs. This movement of continents would of course resulted in much mountain-building activity which in turn would have changed the environment considerably, but for a vast time-scale the heavy Dinosaurs would have thrived unimpeded in a warm stable environment.

The Dinosaurs remained dominant until their demise at the end of the Cretaceous period, at the mass Extinction when the 'primordial world' came to an end. Yet for 135 million years the Dinosaurs filled the earth. It was during the late Jurassic that our feathered 'Archaeopteryx' appeared, and the first flowering 'Angiosperms', and the first truly humble mammals. But it was at the mass Extinction of 65 that this new life blossomed in an extraordinary way! And not long after that the primates appeared, around 50 million years ago, for by now the stage was set for the eventual coming of Man.

But our concern for now is to look at the 'Big Ten', the story of 'Bronto':

THE BIG TEN

1. "So why did God make the Dinosaurs so incredibly enormous, seemingly out of all proper proportions? What possible meaning and purpose could there be in that!..."

Since God had a task to perform which required an extraordinary amount of labour, yet one which He Himself could not do, He created the Dinosaurs who would be large enough and capable enough to carry it out for Him upon the land-surface of the world.

Imagine a builder with his mate, who had to lay a concrete slab. If it was a small area they might mix by hand, but if it was the size of a football pitch, then he would need to commission a fleet of Ready-Mix lorries to do the work for him. Alternatively, he could have employed ten thousand labourers to mix and lay by hand, but for the sake of efficiency (and the curing process) our builder would get on the phone and open his pocket!

In other words, the size of the job is in direct proportion to the method used. Apart from which, time matters, and there are other works to be done after the slab is laid and done.

The Dinosaurs were enormous simply because the task was enormous and needed that sort of creature to fulfil God's purposes. Indeed, I expect that no land animal could subsist in this world larger than the Dinosaurs, notwithstanding that there were many different shapes and sizes, of herbivores, omnivores and carnivores. But if we compare an adult elephant which weighs up to 8 tons and is about 7 metres long, with that of the larger Herbivorous Dinosaurs (Sauropods), many of which weighed 40 to 100 tons and more, and measured from 20 to 40 metres long, we may then get our sense of proportions right! So we may conclude that God went to extremes, putting enormous strains upon bone and tissue, all in order to accomplish a most important task which would ultimately change the face of the earth.

Furthermore, their size and the length of their necks meant that even the tops of trees could be foraged readily. But another aspect to this foraging would be the huge impact upon the environment, for they were not delicate eaters, but indiscriminate in every way, tearing down, uprooting and stripping without a care in the world! This bad behaviour is exactly what God wanted so that vast quantities of plant material would litter the ground and be trampled to bits.

An enormous task demands a bigger than life solution, and only creatures the stature and habits of the Dinosaurs could possibly accomplish it.

2. "So, if the task was carried out by giants, then why did it take all of 135 million years to complete?"

This is to do with the nature of the task which was threefold. The first was to consume as much vegetation as was physically possible. The second was the need to range thoroughly over the entire world, over and over again. And the third was to facilitate abundant seed dispersal. Clearly, the balance of nature had to be just right to keep in step with these heavyweights.

Needless to say, when a herd of these creatures are grazing, consuming everything in their path, leaving a wave of destruction behind them, what remained needed time to regenerate enough to be eaten again. This would take a long time, especially for the conifers. Meanwhile, those eaters had moved on to greener pastures, moving freely around a flat Pangaea, and after the formation of continents, the same would apply but with distinct differences facilitating diversity. After all, they must have moved extremely slowly yet eating up just about everything around them.

Of course, God was particularly keen for His flowering Angiosperms to multiply and diversify throughout the world, and the Dinosaurs assisted to make this happen, not simply due to dispersal of seeds but more importantly to provide the perfect dung-conditions for germination.

But what was essentially needed was to create a general top-soil suitable for purpose, and for this God needed 135 million years to attain such soil conditions as were demanded for our Angiosperms upon which mammals and birds and insects would so much depend. Furthermore, mammals would not appreciate Pangaea, nor the birds, nor even the flowering plants. These three kingdoms of life require a far more diverse and seasonal environment to stimulate growth and prosperity!

Spreading 'muck' and making 'compost' and building mountains and moving continents all takes enormous amounts of time, especially as we are speaking about the entire land mass of the world! Needless to say, those heavy Sauropods were not too pleased with all this change: imagine trying to climb a hillside to get to your food when you weigh 50+ tons!

3. The KTR

The Dinosaurs diversified in abundance during the first third of their history, and the Jurassic was like a haven during which they enjoyed total dominance. But, against all scientific predictions, during the last third of their history, the Dinosaurs stubbornly refused to 'adapt'. Why? When everything was beckoning to them to diversify and change, all the evidence suggests that Bronto remained the same. Indeed, Bronto was dominant one minute and extinct the next!

The period between 125 to 80 million years ago is marked especially by Palaeontologists by the grand title of 'The Cretaceous Terrestrial Revolution' (KTR). The reason why they mark it out is because life was undergoing an extraordinary degree of diversification on the land. From out of Pangaea's monotype 'flat' existence, the dispersal of the continents meant that a new set of dynamics were at work. The environmental picture of mountains, rivers, plains and valleys, meant that the newly emerging flowering plants, insects, birds, and mammals could diversify, and did so most profoundly. The Revolution, so called, is exactly what it says, a rapidly expanding world of new and varied life forms. Under these circumstances, one would expect our dominant friend to keep in step with things and to 'adapt', but he did not. That is despite the fact that the Dinosaurs had reached their peak of diversity exactly during this KTR period. But the evidence indicates no shift either way, neither progress nor decline, in terms of meeting these new demands. Bronto just kept on doing the same old thing, 'to graze and raze', that is, despite a revolution going on all around him! Just imagine all that new succulent leafy matter, delicate, requiring a delicate touch; imagine all that extra nutrition of fruit growing on the steep hillsides. The fact is that Bronto was not made for the delicate touch, he was not made for the slopes, nor given the intelligence to adapt, he was not meant for that! Meanwhile, however, an array of new more complex life had appeared onto the scene, fit and very happy to meet the demands of the new ever-changing seasonal environment. The world was on the verge of a complete transformation which saw out the Dinosaurs.

God had transformed the vast deserty place of Pangaea during the Triassic, to become a Dino-haven in the Jurassic. But one might say that during the Cretaceous period, His attention was firmly on the KTR, knowing that everything was now ready, the **bridge** was being built and almost complete, and new life was waiting to enter a new world, the World God for-saw from the beginning.

Like a desert in Nevada which suddenly receives rain, transforming a wasteland into a glorious bloom of life and colour, in like manner, we might say that what followed the Great Extinction was like Noah ushering the animals into a New

World. God knows what He is about, and sees to it that the means fulfils the end for which it was meant. Bronto was the 'means' of bringing in God's ultimate vision for a wondrous World.

4. Farming the primordial way

The seed ferns and Gymnosperms, such as the monkey puzzle tree, first appeared about 380 million years ago. With wind-blown pollen from male organs fertilizing female ovules, which produced resilient seeds able to resist periods of drought, the Triassic dry harsh environment did not hinder these hardy plants from flourishing unimpeded throughout the vast super-continent of Pangaea. Over a period of 180 million years, these plants spread readily to produce forests, and with the forests came more frequent rains, which led to abundance and dominance over the earth. It was now, about 200 million years ago, that the Dinosaurs first appeared, and tucked into the ever present fodder.

After 70 million more years of Dinosaur foraging, the Angiosperms first appeared, diversifying and spreading rapidly, so that within another 60 million years they had become the dominant plant group just prior to the demise of the Dinosaurs. However, God always destined a proper place in the 'New World' for the majestic evergreens. So the Angios and the Gymnos were never in competition, but the Gymnos willingly surrendered their place to the Angios simply because they did not want all that rich soil! Instead, they clung happily to the steep rocky hillsides and sandy places, the rugged peaks and ice-cold latitudes for which they were intended and where no self-respecting Angio would ever be found.

Now, while conifers enjoy growing in the meanest of soils, not so the Angiosperms! Give a conifer some sand, a few boulders, and some scraps of mulch litter blown by the wind into cracks and crevices and the occasional water, and the seed will germinate and grow into a mighty tree. But not so the Flowering Plants, not so! For they require far more nutrients to support them, to satisfy their needs.

Now, the Earth was poor in those primordial days, that is, until the Dinosaurs came along. For by their manner, their behaviour, and their diet, they not only trampled into the ground millions of tons of plant and woody material which was then broken down by those friendly fungi and bacteria to form **compost**, but of course, they also deposited millions of tons of **manure** into the bargain. These two constituents make up the essential ingredient and texture of a nutrient-rich soil, capable of retaining moisture and providing a fit ground for the Angiosperms to grow.

Yes, the Conifers dominate the sands and every harsh place, even today, but the flowering plants dominate the fertile soils. And so if we look again at the fossil records, we find that the Angiosperms found a foothold after the Dinosaur had done their work for 70 million years, and became the dominant plant group after another 60 million years. That is to say, by virtue of the Dinosaurs composting and spreading muck for more than 125 million years, we have the necessary soil conditions in place to transform to world!

Now, that is a long time, and it seems to me that if we do our calculations correctly, we should discover that those hard working Dinosaurs accomplished their task by then, of spreading a mixture of compost and manure to the required depth across the entire landmass into which they were sent.

If we look again at our 'football pitch' and the 'Ready-Mix' workers, and we multiple this by the factor of 'Bronto' and the Earth, and we replace the fork with the hoof and add compost into the equation, spread over the entire surface of the Earth, then what do we get? By my reckoning, that comes to just the right amount for our Angiosperms to enjoy! The Good Gardener knows His business, even if the tools He must use belong to a primordial world. And we know from our own experience that the Gardener ensures that His labourer does a good job (so long as they are willing!), which is why I have declared Bronto to be the Heavyweight Champion of the World!

But let us not forget the wonderful part played by Bronto in transporting seeds so far and wide, deposited in just the right way for germination. This is of immense importance and has remained so ever since, among the birds and the mammals that have followed Bronto's example.

So let's look a moment at the calculation, since size is directly proportional to end product.

The African farmer is well aware of the value to him of elephant dung, but sadly, has very little access to use it for his fields. I am told that the average amount of dung a single elephant drops per day is about 80kg. 10,000 elephants therefore produce 800,000kg which is 800 tons. An African elephant weighs 7.5 tons, whereas the average Sauropod weighed about 75 tons. So if 10,000 elephants produce 800 tons of dung per day, that means that the equivalent number of Dinosaurs would have produced about 80,000 tons per day (and that's a conservative estimate). Together with this calculation for manure produced, we must of course include into the equation the vast quantities of vegetal and tree debris, of compost produced. The final outcome spread over a period of 125 million years of dinosaur domination, over a land surface of 150 million square kilometres should work out just right! As for working out the maths, alas, I'm afraid I fall short of the mark!

5. Quality and quantity

So let's look at the product, for the farmer has used a combination of *bedding material* and *animal manure* to fertilize his soil for growing his crops since time immemorial. Manure is probably the best soil improver of all, BUT it needs to be well-rotted and needs a skilful hand to do so. The muck heap needs to be big enough so as not to dry out, and it needs to be fibrous enough for air to get in, otherwise the biological process will not take place. Now, whereas the farmer is at liberty to muck-in and get his hands dirty, God is not, but must rely on Bronto to do the work for Him. However, since God is the Skilled Gardener, He knows that Bronto is fit for purpose in so many ways.

Indeed, the gardener explains that whereas compost is best applied sparingly to get the best effect, manure (if properly made) can be added at high volumes, improving the soil with each application. Indeed, apparently you can never have enough of it, for the plants for which it was meant will thrive, make further demands and beg for more! Furthermore, that when mixed into the green waste, the manure acts as an activator, speeding up the process of composting plant material. The gardener warns us however, that the disadvantage with farmyard manure is that it invariably contains lots of seeds (of weeds), but of course for God's purposes, that's exactly what He wanted from old Bronto... dispersing a variety of seeds all over the world!

Fossilized Coprolites tells us a little about what Dinosaurs ate, but it appears that most of these finds are from Carnivores. But what we want to find out here, is more to do with the Herbivores because they were responsible for the vast proportion of manure and composting production. So the best we can do is to look at the elephant and the horse for clues, because they both consume a lot yet have poor digestive abilities. For example, the elephant consumes as much as 300kg of plant matter in a day, eating about 5 percent of their bodyweight, and yet only 50 percent of the ingested food gets digested! The horse also has poor digestive ability, and we may well assume the same for the Sauropods. Furthermore, the elephant defecates up to 18 times in a 16-18 hour working day, spread over perhaps 10 to 20kms. In other words, almost 80 percent of what elephants eat returns to the ground as potentially highly fertile manure. I say 'potentially' because there are a number of important factors which go into making good quality manure, as any good gardener will tell you. If the pile is too small and dries up quickly, it is not much good, but if the pile is large enough (or is made so by an outside agent like a farmer!), then it will allow the right conditions for bacterial action and heat generation. However, too much rain will leach out the goodness, but the evidence tends to suggest that during the Jurassic which basked in near tropical splendour, that the climate was not so wet.

We may conclude from these things that Bronto was most suitable for the production of the most valuable product in the garden, mixing up time and again the basis for a rich aerated soil so appreciated by the newly emerging Flowering Plants, AND, may I add, for the diversity of the Fungi which have always been a vital mutual player in the Ecosystem in so many ways.

And let us not forget the vast quantities of bone-meal and blood which adds important ingredients to the mix. Tyrannosaurus and friends would have provided plenty of that over the years!

6. The predator prey balance

Of course, it goes without saying, that all herbivores need their carnivore relatives to keep the balance. Take out the carnivore from the field, and the herbivore will overpopulate and destroy it. In other words, too many Sauropods would eat up too much vegetation and turn the land into desert. So carnivores are a major player in maintaining the optiumum population balance, it's as simple as that.

As for Tyrannosaurus Rex, most famous of all, I must say that he did not play such an important role after all, since his size and weight was much the same as our elephant, even though, like the lion of the African savannah, he must have roared his presence most fiercely! Any old or lame Sauropods must have been easy prey for him, but then again, life for a lame animal is no life at all, so maybe it's best if we see T Rex as an agent of compassion rather than the popular notion of killer!

7. Pangaea: the primordial homeland

Whereas the Dinosaurs enjoyed Pangaea, the same could not be said of the Mammals, the Birds, and the Angiosperms all of which wanted to find a variety of different habitats which Pangaea did not provide. This was a place for the Primordial and not for the Modern. So when the super-continent of Pangaea finally broke up (according to God's intervention and will), this changed the balance in favour of the latter. Even so, when it did brake up 175 million years ago, it did so into two continents: Laurasia and Gondwana, which the Dinosaurs would be agreeable with, until they broke up again about 145 million years ago into a variety of continents of different characters similar to today.

But Pangaea was home, and God made sure that they had all the comforts of home, easy to get around with that massive weight to bear. Flat and abundant in food to satisfy even the biggest appetite, that is, as soon as the hot dry Triassic had given way to the humid warm climate of the Jurassic. It seems, however, that by the Cretaceous period, those relaxing days were to be replaced with much more pronounced climatic variation and fluctuation (as planned by God), which suited very well the diversification of new plants and animals in preparation for the 'New World' that was soon to come, a world that was not meant for the Dinosaurs at all.

8. Extinction has meaning

The time of the Dinosaur was unique. For never has there been an animal Group which came into being, diversified into every shape and size, herbivorous, omnivorous and carnivorous, which dominated the scene so completely and yet came to such a complete end. Like a work of science fiction that all happened in a forgotten space and time, with only fossils to declare to us their existence. While every other living Group of animals has living cousins to tell their tale to us today, (even the amphibians, the first land vertebrates, who moved onto the land some 370 million years ago, have the frogs to tell us their tale), we find that the Dinosaurs have only a sub-group to tell their tale. So dominant and diverse, yet T. Rex and his cousins must point indignantly at their small flighty cousins once-removed! And there's an obvious and ironic contradiction in terms: that Dinosaurs, with feet so firmly on the ground, should be responsible for the origin of such a swift flighty dancer of the skies! So even though the birds of today sing their song for us to hear, I doubt that *they remember* from whence they came!

So, besides the birds, we could say that the Dinosaurs are an enigma, for they came, they conquered, and they died. A bit like so many civilisations, you might say!

However, there is indeed meaning in the madness, as I have been at pains to explain, how they fulfilled a most indispensable task in laying the groundwork for the 'New World' to come. And there is no doubt that they accomplished their commission very well, since we are here today, able to tell their tale for them.

Indeed, the uniqueness of the Dinosaur surely adds weight to my hypothesis, that God brings everything into being for good purpose, and He brings things to an end for equally good purpose. He is in charge, directing the entire field of play, carrying out His immutable will unto its preordained goal.

So when we hear that the Dinosaurs were wiped out in the Extinction of 65, we know that there is meaning and purpose in that, since the flip-side of this Event led to the extraordinary blossoming of life as never before seen on the Earth, an explosion of diversity of every living thing that was meant to survive the cataclysmic meteor impact that God sent. The 'Primordial World had ended, and the 'New World' had begun, the last stage towards the Perfect outcome *that is still to come.*

9. Dinosaur: origin of the Birds

One of the most miraculous works of evolutionary creation is the creation of the Birds. I include the birds into my Ten because without the Dinosaurs the world would not have been blessed with birds.

When we speak about the origin of the birds, we are compelled to ponder the miraculous: the sudden appearance in the fossil record of a winged creature dressed in feathers, designed to almost perfection for flight, precision engineering that leaves one speechless when you consider that this happened all of a sudden during the time of the Dinosaurs over 150 million years ago.

Archaeopteryx and her cousins show us that the first steps to flight was no tentative measure with a string of improvements along the way, but in fact an extraordinary metamorphoses from scales and barbs and spiny things upon the skins of Dinosaurs, recreated and transformed into a sophisticated array of feathers arranged in perfect unison upon a fit for purpose wing. OK, Archaeo was a little heavy and clumsy in the air, but what a leap into the unknown! And OK, those flying Pterosaurs like Pterodactyl may have helped our Archaeo with the idea, but who gave her the wings?

Let's for a moment look at those fossil wings because they look to me like the real thing! Plumage with interlocking barbs to anchor the plums in formation, ordered in perfect asymmetric sequence to a curved aerofoil wing perfectly designed for flight with plumed tail to match.

So how on earth can science hold to that adage of mutant genes playing that random game to come up with perfection in one almighty moment of chance?! The consensus holds that it is due to rare chance genetic mutations in DNA, (that raw material of evolutionary change), that a given creature is provided with new physiological opportunities for adapting to a new set of environmental demands. But I say that is an absurd assumption, even taking into account 'probabilities' over a vast time-scale. The feather does indeed have its origin wrapped up in DNA change, but such engineering cannot be by chance but by design. Such a chance event would be like waving a wand over a 'T Ford' and begetting a F1 racing car!

However, it is most probable as suggested by Palaeontologists, that Archaeo has her origins with the Theropods of which T. Rex is one. Of course there were many smaller more nimble Theropods, bird-like in manner, hopping and chasing about catching insects and the like, but its difficult to imagine them trying to catch the wind for take-off!

Be that as it may, I am convinced that God always had in mind the creation of the Birds, and that the Dinosaurs were therefore indispensable for this purpose, for it is surely they that provided the necessary *genetic information* for the Creator to work with in bringing about the Birds. So, we may conclude that the Dinosaurs not only gave us the **fertile soil** to bless the ground at our feet, but also they gave us the **birds** to grace our skies!

And after all, where would the birds roost and make their nest safely if not in the thickets of thorny shrubs and the highest branches of trees? And what would our Aerial friends do for food if not for the abundance provided of fruit and seed and the array of insect to be found in those unreachable heights where only they can go. Of course, God had in mind the skills of primate and ultimately the intelligence of Man to reap the blessing of the Angiosperm in so many ways. Yet, in a wonderful and interdependent way, Bird and Tree share a common bond of necessity, together, with the array of insect. No, the world would be no good at all without them all, and that's a fact!

All this new dynamic of complex life was ripe and ready to explode into action at 65 with the coming of the 'New World' so well prepared by the Dinosaurs.

So surely we see now why Bronto is our Champion!

10. 'Ten' belongs to GOD

This number belongs to God for two reasons: firstly, because 'ten' refers to the completion of a set numeral system (decimal), just as seven refers to the completion of a set period of time (a week). The evolutionary Work done by God was over 'six days', and on the 'seventh' (which completes the full unit of time) "God ceased from all His work". (Genesis 2:2)

But as Saint Peter the fisherman tells us, "With the Lord a day is like a thousand years, and a thousand years are like a day". (ref.2 Peter 3:8) So if a fisherman from Galilee over two thousand years ago understood this much, how much more should we be able to understand the symbolic meaning given by Scripture for something which back then they could not know about as we do today! There are those who cling too literally to what is written rather than allowing God to open up for them the deeper meaning of His Word, but how rudely many 'unbelievers' like to mock this profound symbol of time written for our deeper understanding!

What matters here is to recognise that God's **evolutionary Work** was accomplished in six days, "Thus the heavens and the earth were completed in all their vast array". (ref. Genesis 2:1)"By the seventh day God had finished the work He had been doing, so He rested". (Genesis 2:2)

So, this is where I stand: that ever since Adam and Eve entered the Garden of Eden ready to meet their Maker (and to receive the final and most important blessing of all), ever since that historic moment in time and place, the dynamic for change that we call 'evolution' came to an end. In other words, what we have seen and discovered ever since that moment is on the back of a different *dynamic for change* mostly as a result of pressures between humans and Nature in a 'fallen world'.

The second reason why this number belongs to God is because the World still awaits **'The Fulfilment'** when God Himself shall intervene and establish the World according to His pre-ordained Plan. It is for Man's sake alone that this delay was necessary (because of our Fall from grace in that Garden), for God did not make us to live this autonomous life as we experience today, but He made us uniquely for Himself, to be bound by a **Covenant of Love**, to live our lives in His Holy Company, in obedience, faithfulness and truth. So all life awaits that Day when God will bring the World to its rightful and most blessed conclusion. (ref. Romans 8: 19–23)

CONCLUSIONS

Having studied the 'Ten' with you and seen how essential the Dinosaurs were in bringing about the 'New World', I hope that you have seen how the evolutionary journey of life on earth was under the providential guidance of the Almighty according to a *blueprint* rather than a string of random chance episodes in which species must compete in a mutually selfish struggle for existence, to adapt, move on or perish.

But more than this, what I want to make clear is my conviction that Man's encounter with his Creator in the Garden of Eden was a defining moment, the very moment when 'evolution' *per se* came to an end. For "God saw all that He had made, and it was very good". (Genesis 1:31) This closed the chapter on God's 'evolutionary' Work, and so the *dynamic for change* thereafter should not be seen in the same light. Indeed, that Moment in the Garden was meant to be the transforming climax for the whole earth, because God's immutable intention was to enter into and make His home with us forever, (see. John 14:23) blessing all creation by His Presence. Alas, this Moment has yet to be realised because of Man's fall from grace in that Garden, and so it is in this light that we hear Saint Paul declare that, "the creation itself became subjected to frustration, not by its own choice but by the Will of the One who subjected it, in the hope that the creation will (one day) be liberated from its bondage to decay..." (ref. Romans 8:20) So rather than being on an evolutionary journey towards its pre-ordained goal, the living world must now await to be finally liberated. This is the Christian mystery of the 'Kingdom of God'- "the world that is to come".

Saint Paul also tells us that the world is imbued with "God's invisible qualities – His eternal power and Divine Nature" (ref. Romans 1:20) – and since the essence of God's Nature may be defined as the perfection of *uncreated* 'Beauty' and 'Love', then it follows from this that He fashioned and imbued His World to manifest and to reflect this twofold truth. And since man and woman are made in God's image and likeness, we are created to reflect that Beauty and Love most perfectly. Furthermore, as already hinted at, Nature herself displays these qualities most perfectly by her innately intimate sensual and sexual nature. This then is Nature's truest Image in glory to her Creator. The fact that Man has '**fallen**' from his perfect virtue and nobility, dragging down the natural world with him, (ref. Genesis 3:17 and 6:13) means that the Work of God is not yet finished, for God must ultimately **redeem** us to Himself before He can declare truly, "when God saw all that He had made, it was VERY GOOD". (ref. Genesis 1:31)

That day fast approaches when God will finally have His way, whether we like it or not. However, herein lies the Mystery: that this world is imbued with the intimacy of sex in so many wonderful ways. In the Kingdoms of Evergreen and Flowering Plants, male and female, in colourful splendour and form, bound together by the wind and upon the touch of a wing. In the Kingdom of the Birds, with their courtship rituals and song, their exquisite plumage and dance, and their social affinity, following the seasons for that special moment called Spring. In the Kingdom of the Mammals, male and female, eagerly sniffing the air for signs, playing out their lives for this unrivalled moment, to find and to mate. Of course, for Man who is made uniquely to be in fellowship with his Creator, we are called to glorify God through LOVE, bearing the fruit of Divine Love and filling the house with gladness! And it is to this mystery of Love awakened in Man at the dawn of his existence that I tell our own story in Part Two.

Now there are those from both the Religious and Scientific camps who say: 'SEX... is but the necessary means of procreation in this life (which has no place in the life to come); SEX... is for reproduction, passing on genes, an impulse of species survival'. But I must reply to them all: 'It appears that you have put aside the aspiration of the heart to realise true happiness! For the Psalmist raises his voice to us and says',

"Delight yourselves in the Lord and He will give you the desires of your heart".

(Psalm 37:4)

Indeed, God created all the living things, male and female, "to keep their various kinds alive throughout the earth", (ref. Genesis 7:3) "**But**," said the Lord God to the man, "**I have established My Covenant with you,**" (ref. Genesis 6:18) "male and female, made in My own image and likeness." (ref. Genesis 1:26)

Be it said, that among all the creatures that God made, <u>we are the most sexual</u>, made perfectly for Love's intimate and naked embrace just as our Creator intended. It is this aspect of our being covenanted to God which makes us truly human.

Jesus turned 'water into wine'. (John 2:11) Mary's womb was fertilized by the Spirit of God, and the Son of God was born into the world. And by the power of the Spirit of God, Jesus' body which lay in death after His Crucifixion was **_raised_** into Divinity, resurrected to **eternal life**, body and soul. And to all who believe and hope in their heart in this 'True Man and True God', we too shall follow Him into the World that is to come.

Genesis has laid the foundation; God has given His Invitation; but it is up to each one of us to accept it or not.

PART TWO

HUMAN ORIGINS

PREFACE

When I was young I was confronted with the scientific view that life has its origins in some primordial alchemy of nature, and that as such, humankind itself is the outcome of the developmental process of evolution rooted in this accepted theory! I soon realised that the Scientific Community has no regard at all for the alternative model based upon the existence of God, of Divinity acting in and upon the natural world to bring about a preordained outcome. But what distressed me most of all was their almost casual acceptance that the mystery of LOVE itself must also find its roots in Nature rather than from up above! (see 1 John 4:7) And in those days, I was simply an agnostic.

To be sure, I am not alone in my abhorrence of this scientific explanation of Life, of Humanity, and of Love! Indeed, such a one-sided model is divorced from Man's highest good, namely, the life-giving principle of LOVE which in fact defines our humanity. The very word 'humanity' has become synonymous with 'one who loves', so it is only when this Profound Mystery is given centre stage that true understanding is possible.

So the story I have told herein does this: it collects the fragments from under our feet and listens to the commentary given, then it takes this knowledge before God, looking for an answer. In this way, what was in the dark is illuminated by the Light and a meaningful Picture is revealed, bringing concurrence between these two fundamentally distinct realms of knowledge – of Science and Religion. For it is only when we see the twofold nature of our being – biological and spiritual – that we are then enabled to understand what is before our eyes. This then, is the essential current of my thoughts as I follow our Ancestor upon his journey into maturity, to then enter the Garden of Eden and the Presence of God as told by the Book of Genesis.

My endeavour, therefore, is to recover the ground between Research and Revelation, allowing empirical knowledge to assist me to make sense of and piece together the story presented by the Bible; for in no wise can I avoid either the resolve of my Faith which stands upon Divine Revelation, nor to side-step the Archaeological findings of our past.

So, with my Bible to enlighten, my premise from 'Part One', and my reference book* for 'Part Two' to lead me to encounter our Ancestor, I hope that, God willing, I shall unravel the past, notwithstanding the essential matter of my Testimony in which I reveal the mystery of man's union with God, opening the door to true understanding.

My task then is to fit the pieces of the puzzle together so that it makes sense and reason of the archaeological records, yet remains faithful and true to Scripture, for I will have it no other way!

*"The Human Past: World Prehistory &
the Development of Human Society" edited
by Chris Scarre, Thames & Hudson 2005

STORY OF OUR ANCESTOR

Clearly, unlike the story of Bronto, we must come much closer to home, yet, as if coming to my aid again, I am met with another anomaly of giants and extinctions centred upon the last Ice Age, which began about 70,000 years ago and ended about 10,000 years ago. And as I said before, such things are not by chance, but are full of meaning, how this extreme period of the earth's history should co-inside so perfectly with the emergence and spread of Homo sapiens out of Africa into a chilling environment of land and beast! What I hope to do then, is to follow their journey to see where it takes us, and eventually, even into the Garden of Eden.

A bone to pick with the theologian

But before I begin, I must pick a bone with those theologians who are so happy to turn everything into metaphor! For I hold rigidly to Paul's vision; I hold rigidly to the Christian doctrine of Adam's transgression, and his descendants consequential inheritance of a 'sinful nature' in need of Redemption; I hold rigidly to the orthodox understanding of 'Original Sin' and the Fall from grace that took place in the Garden planted by God in Eden. (ref. Genesis 2:8) And this means that Adam and Eve must be regarded as historical persons as depicted by Scripture. Even the genealogy of Jesus is traced back to Adam by Luke, the distinguished Doctor of sense and reason! Then there is the question of the man that God had *'formed'*, (meaning, not merely in body but in mind and heart also, which required schooling), who God summoned to enter the Garden. Scripture tells us that this Garden was situated between the rivers Tigris and the Euphrates. Furthermore, I want to make clear that the **'innocence of man'** prior to the Fall is highly significant from the moral perspective; and that after the Fall, the evidence shows the sudden appearance of all the behavioural traits one would expect of **'sinful man'** as recounted in Scripture.

I. Hominins and the emergence of MAN

To begin our story, we must go to Africa, to the birthplace of all Hominins, the earliest members of proto-human lineage (not origins), who lived in Africa between 2 and 6 million years ago.

As we know from Part One, Mammals became the dominant land animal from 65 million years ago. From primate diversity came the Hominidae, and from them came the bipedal Hominins, appearing perhaps as far back as 6 million years ago, in the areas of south, east, and central Africa. *'Australopithecus'* is the most famous of these early hominins, who were already using simple stone tools even as early as 2.5 million years ago. Then from 2 to 1.7 million years ago we see the early emergence of the genus 'Homo', such as *'Homo rudolfensis'*, *'habilis'*, and *'ergaster'*. From here we encounter the appearance of **'Homo erectus'**, **'Homo neanderthalensis'**, and **'Homo sapiens'**, dating from 1 million years ago, 400,000 years and 350,000 years respectively. At about 50,000 years ago (and earlier) both 'Homo neanderthalensis' and 'Homo sapiens' dispersed into Eurasia from out of Africa. From the evidence, these peoples travelled far and wide across the globe, reaching Australia about 40,000 years ago. But our focus will be with those who remained in Eurasia, since I wish to discover the origins of Adam and Eve in the Garden, between the rivers Tigris and the Euphrates.

Also, at some time before this, 'Homo Erectus' had taken his journey into the wider world, but records show that he died out about the same time as his distant cousins set off on their own adventure. Then Neanderthalensis died out about 30,000 years ago, leaving Homo sapiens to dominate the field. Just to say here, that Homo ergaster also did his dispersal and spread into the wider world much earlier, but we are only concerned with the direct lineage and origin of Man – Homo sapiens.

What matters to us in our search is to see evidence of not just stone tools commonly used by so many Hominins, but also other artefacts synonymous with *historical* hunter-gatherer traits which would include cultural behaviour, the use of language and artistic expression, the use of fire for cooking, the making of utensils and the construction of shelters and dwellings, ceremonial burial etc, all which we would expect of true humans. These findings suddenly start appearing in East Africa **at 50,000 years ago**, and show up again in the Levantine Corridor (the regions of Syria, Lebanon and Israel, which formed a major corridor for human and faunal movements between Africa and Eurasia), at *Qafzeh* in Israel from around 35,000 years ago, telling us that, by this time, these peoples had already embarked upon establishing settlements in a completely new climate and environment demanding new invention and creative skills.

Most importantly, the appearance of 'syntax' language as opposed to simple speech is the mark of modern man, which opened up his world beyond mere subsistence. Without this faculty, we would not be who we are, and research into the genetic origins of language has opened up our understanding of the past.

Perhaps the most compelling evidence for our 'bench mark' date for true human beginnings, therefore, is found in genetic DNA research which identified one specific 'FOXP2' *gene mutation* derived on the 'Y' male chromosome some time after 100,000 years ago which biologically facilitated <u>language</u> as we know it. Initially, as I understand it, this was a male faculty, but that over time, females would have acquired this by means of imitation and participation. In a wonderful way, therefore, men and women were drawn together to cooperate side by side in an intimate way in order to **share** this most essential faculty, the man leading the woman to explore the wonder of language and the sharing of ideas.

My reference book states in this regard, "**This mutation supports the belief of Paul Mellars (1989) and Richard Klein (1995) that behavioural modernity originated relatively suddenly in Africa around 50,000 years ago and spread rapidly from there**." (quoted from *The Human Past: World Prehistory & the Development of Human Society'*).

What I have presented here is only a simplified background of a much more complicated picture, but it gives an ample idea before we turn our attention to the last Ice Age into which our Homo sapiens were to go...

II. MAN 'called' into the land of snow and ice

You may think that there cannot be much meaning and purpose in being 'called' to go where hardship and struggle were bound to direct the course of our lives. But just as it is said that conflict is the mother of all invention, so too, conflict with the elements and the beasts draws out in man every necessary skill and invention just to survive. There is no place for idleness in an Ice Age! And it is also said that a time of shared conflict and struggle draws people closer together, supporting one another. So there is only work and fellowship to cling to in an Ice Age, and this was the very reason why God sent the last Ice Age: He sent it for the education of man!

So these pioneers opening up new lands of opportunity did so against the current of good sense! They encountered a remarkably unstable cold climate with an austere living environment to match! Nevertheless, these people cut trails deep into the icy grasslands of the north, where vast ice-sheets formed the horizon. These were the lands of the Ice Age, into which the extraordinary Ice Age mammals lived, hunted, and grazed. The cave lion, biggest lion that ever lived, 3.5 metres long. These huge felines probably hunted in a similar way as today's lions. The woolly mammoth, 3 tons or more, with 4 metre long tusks. The saber-toothed cats, with larger than life canine teeth, preying on mammoth, rhinos and other thick skinned animals. And then there were the other herbivores, the giant deer, the aurochs, horse, and deer which ranged over the grassy steppes. All these great animals of the Ice Age were reverently and meaningfully painted with the finesse of a true artist by our ancestors, upon cave walls so deep, dark and mysterious. There is little doubt that this rich fauna gave great incentive to man, who enjoyed the hunt and its rewards. So men went with their families after the prey as these animals migrated across the seasonal lands in search of fodder. Obviously, there were other important foods for our ancestors to gather and harvest from the wilds, but meat (cooked meat) was the vital ingredient and nourishment for them, worth the risks, despite the presence of so many fearful beasts. Just imagine hunting the mammoth with spears, and hauling all that meat and hides (dried or otherwise) back home over the tundra for days and days, and keeping watch for the cave lion who kept close on your tail, burning fires around the camp at night for protection and keeping the ember going by day! Life was on the edge... once you leave home and adventure out into an unknown land. How many of us there are throughout history who have done the same, carrying our children with us against the tide of good sense! Intrepid is what we are, and our ancestors were too.

But life for them was not simply a matter of tending to their nutritional needs. Life for man has always been far more expansive and creative than that! And so we find profound symbolic imagery in the cave paintings, the carved images upon bone and ivory. Everything became decorated, measured in design and purpose. Social networks and settlements increased and marked seasons would make further demands as lifestyle became more sophisticated and complex with every day. Also, the interglacial warmer periods and freezing glacial maximums during the Ice Age meant repeated migrations, as populations had to abandon the north to take refuge in southern climes, only to return north a few generations later. This meant a lot of social interaction and diversity, sharing one another's knowledge, experiences, and ideas. Settlements increased in size, leading to further integration of larger groups of people, which in turn would demand greater order and discipline to ensure social harmony was maintained. But in all the archaeological findings from this period (until the end of the Ice Age) identified with modern humans, I am led to believe that there is a complete absence of any evidence that would suggest the presence of violent and social conflict between these people. For my belief is that Man in those days lived in a state of innocence in that his heart was **humble, true and honest**, and no malice or lie was to be found in him. That is not to say that people did not get into a tussle once in a while, but that the guiding ethos was of reconciling peace. As we shall find, however, the period after 10,000 years ago shows a different kettle of fish, with mighty defences, mighty Kings, and mighty Cities, indicative of greed, rivalry, pride, and every wickedness under the sun!

III. Man shepherded to GOD

There is every reason to believe that Neanderthals lived alongside humans for a considerable time. Both were competent with tools and hunted the same prey. But whereas the Neanderthals kept to caves and set off on the hunt from these permanent homes and hearths, settling according to the potential foraging and tolerable hunting range around them and beholden to the presence of caves to make their home in, our ancestors were free from these constraints, not beholden to caves but ingeniously built their own shelters and homes with whatever suitable raw materials were available, like branches, stones, hides, and even bones. Such flexibility and impermanence of home meant that they could follow the seasonal migrations of the herds and set up camp at will. Hunting parties could set off for long distances and set up temporary shelters, spending time to prepare their game for drying and storage before returning to the permanent settlement far away. Nevertheless, I can just imagine the women back home anxiously grumbling among themselves, "why are they away so long? Why did we come to this bone-chilling land? Surely we were better off in Africa!" But for all this difficulty, the women would be hard at work foraging around among the plants, tubers, and berries that were to be found roundabout, and seeing to the endless needs of the fire. They would keep the fires burning and care for the children, ensuring the 'home' was in health and order, and learning ever increasing knowledge and uses of medicinal plants, herbs and such like.

Everything was a learning curve for the men and for the women, and Nature provided the backdrop. Yet what was unknown to these people, our true ancestors, was the fact that God, who carried them away into this chill world, by His grace was teaching them what it is to be Human. This seems to be indicated by Scripture, for God says, **"I, the Divine Craftsman, was filled with delight day after day, rejoicing always in His [the Father's] presence, rejoicing**

in His whole world, and delighting in mankind". (Proverbs 8:30-31)

Now, we know only too well that God certainly did <u>not</u> delight in us since our Fall from grace in the Garden! Indeed, He was so grieved in His heart about how wicked we had become, that He determined to wipe mankind from the face of the earth... but Noah found favour in His sight. (ref. Genesis 6:5–8) So we have this extended period of ascent of mankind up to the time that God appeared to Adam in the Garden of Eden. During tens of thousands of years our ancestors lived a life of innocence, during which **abiding grace** would guide and lead and teach and inspire them to ever greater knowledge and understanding. After all, our human ancestors had just left their basic thinking behind, and were given the faculty of language, of cognition and creativity to work on, to share and to learn. This takes a long time, it takes adventure, hardship and endurance, a chill air and a snowflake!

What we need to realise is that man was made uniquely to have a full, personal, and intimate Relationship with his Creator. Coming out of Africa like a child, our ancestors required a long passage of time of schooling in order to attain to spiritual maturity and understanding, and God gave him a harsh environment for his learning. After his schooling was over, now ready and prepared to meet his Maker, God called them away from the dying tundra, He called a man and a woman to meet with Him... in the Garden.

But imagine a mathematician trying to converse algebra with a child! He knows that he must wait until the child has matured and learnt to read algebra before he can meaningfully converse about such things. Likewise, God led man to learn, so that eventually he would be ready to converse and understand the appearing of his Creator before him, for, as Scripture says, "**I will show Myself to him**", (ref. John 14:21) and, "If he loves Me, he will obey My teaching. My Father will love him, and **We will come to him and make Our HOME with him**". (John 14:23) Alas, Adam did not obey and did not keep this Divine Anointing, and from that very moment our ancestors lost innocence and found sin.

So, from out of Africa we were 'called' by God, and we obeyed our calling in those days... and we learnt to care and to love one another. For man was not made like the animals, but was born to be educated and to learn the ways of love. No simple life would suffice for him, which is why he was called out of Africa, called to question the unknown and to wonder about existence and the heavens above; called to use his intelligence and his imagination, to allow inspired thought to move him, to discover the spiritual side of his nature caught up in the mystery of life itself. So for this reason God called His people out of Africa and sent them into the Ice Age on purpose, with grace in abundance to deliver them, for Man was immature, innocent and unschooled and needed to develop his heart and his mind, becoming mature as God intended.

IV. The uniqueness of Man

Ever since the first bipedal Hominins appeared there has been evidence of some sort of stonework. Oldowan industry is characterised by simple core forms of stone tools, but as time went by, hominins developed ever greater skill and new techniques in the use of stone. By 300,000 years ago, high levels of skill and symmetry have been found, and even the use of mineral pigments (ochre), although we do not know for what purpose these pigments were used. But all hominin activity before 50,000 years ago show a complete absence of art, they all failed to build any structure(s), and there is an absence of any refined handwork of bone, ivory or antler. Indeed, generally speaking, hominins differ little other than the successive advances in their hunting and associated stone-working skills. But here is the crux of the matter, quote, **"Archaeologists agree that the pattern changed sharply after 50,000 years ago, when formal bone artefacts, art, housing remnants, and other items associated with historic hunter-gatherers appeared widely for the first time. It is thus only after 50,000 years ago that fully modern behaviour became firmly established."** (from *'The Human Past: World Prehistory & the Development of Human Society'*). And since there is consensus between us in this all important matter, I am persuaded to think that this was the moment when <u>God made claim to a people to call His own</u> "in His own image and likeness". That is to say, that it was at this moment that God's abundant grace and now abiding 'Holy Spirit' established a people whom we may call our true ancestors like us in every way but sin.

This bench-mark of 50,000 years ago is perhaps put into question by numerous *ochre* fragments found which predate this by at least 15,000 years, bearing geometric *cross-hatch* patterns that one might associate with 'art', such as that found at 'Blombos Cave' in South Africa. But though these etched patterns show intent to give value and significance to a specific stone, I am reluctant to associate this as a work of *creative* art. Nevertheless, it proves clearly that human behaviour was already at its developmental stage, as it were, in preparation for our bench-mark moment of 'enlightened' cognition. Indeed, if we look simply at human morphology, then we must go back to at least 125,000 years ago to encounter our origins. But what is physically apparent does not necessarily give a picture of mental aptitude and awareness! So there is no surprise to see that the biological and anatomical emergence of man predates our 'bench-mark' by a long way. And of course, what is found in the ground is but the outward expression pointing to an inward disposition, and it is the inward disposition that makes us what we are.

However, the all important point I want to make here is this: that along this spiritual developmental journey God must have decided at a particular moment in time and amongst a particular family-group of individuals to intervene into their lives by filling them with His **Holy Spirit** (see Acts 2:4) – the abiding 'Counsellor' to be with them, to guide and to inspire this People upon the Way of Life-in-God, drawing them ever closer into the fullness of truth. (see John 14:17) By the inspiration of the Holy Spirit, therefore, this Family of God (unknown to themselves at the time) would be led upon a spiritual journey of maturing and of **becoming fully human**, just as God purposed from the beginning.

Such an inner-revolution of being, though subtle and gentle, yet would have enlightened their minds and enlivened their hearts to the pre-eminence of LOVE as the guiding force of their lives. Furthermore, this transformation of being would have opened the door to full cognitive and creative aptitude giving our *innocent* Family a special and strong sense of identity. No longer bound by Nature, but free to express their spiritual life in Nature... and nothing would ever be the same again as they embarked upon a new journey of **schooling** led by God their Teacher, (see Proverbs 8:30–35) leading our Family ultimately to the supernatural encounter with the Godhead in the Garden of Eden. (see John 14:21–23) It is in this light that we may understand how and why the Spirit of Truth ('Wisdom') delighted in the presence of mankind, (ref. Proverbs 8:31) since these People were innocent and in harmony with the Divine Will. And as you will see, it has become my conviction that this blessed age of accent and innocence continued until the end of the Ice Age at about 10,000 years ago.

V. A place to make their own

So let us follow a group of these humans, a family of thirty or so individuals, as they make their way through the land from out of Africa. They do not stop at the first opportunity since there are others who inhabit the land, so they move on northward in search of somewhere to call their own. Something stirs them on in hope, for they have heard from others of vast herds in the north. So for months they travel, confident that one day they will find a place to settle in, a land full of herds of deer and horses and opportunity. Then they reach the grassy steppes following the herds in season, and they saw the expanse and knew that this was for them. They found a ravine with its river, and in the safety of the steep banks they built their encampment, from where they would hunt amongst the herds.

And it was not so long before they went after bigger game, to conquer the greatest beast of all, the woolly mammoth. With only spears and cunning they trapped the beast and brought him down. And with his hide, his bones and tusks as trophies, they built their monumental homes out on the steppes. They would be known as 'the mammoth hunters'! What trophy and what esteem! Indeed, over all those centuries our family had grown in stature, becoming skilled and wise, sharing knowledge and ideas with others when they gathered for important festivals. Indeed, God was with them, leading them always, teaching them how to be wise and how to love.

But the time for change had arrived for our family after so many generations, for the ice melted, the mammoths retreated, and the land became empty. In any case, the new generation had become agitated, feeling a compulsion to leave. So they left and headed south from whence they came, with stories they had heard about lands rich in grains and every good thing. To this they set off to find a place amongst communities of people. This was at the end of the Ice Age, about 10,000 years ago, leaving behind forever a way of life that was no more.

This simplified story hints at the work done by God, in developing our family's minds and hearts, for we can be sure that, in that dangerous and icy place, caring for one another was a priority and fashioned their behaviour accordingly. Caring is 'Godly love', and our innocent ancestors living in such extreme conditions would readily understand the value of not just mutual caring but caring *per se*. And since God gave man the compulsion to share ideas and experiences with others, we can be sure that our family would have socialised frequently at moments of 'Gathering' with their distant neighbours. But above all else that God wanted them to learn was the aptitude for LOVE. Yes, love is expressed between many different relationships – friendship, parenthood, family – but without rival is the intimate relationship of 'lovers'. Today, we take sex for granted, but not so for our innocent ancestors for who sex was a new world of discovery! "How so?" you may ask! Because, during those 40,000 years, God was leading our ancestors to experience and explore their sensuality and sex for the very first time. "How so?" You may ask! Because, until then, God had not given of His spiritual Love for our ancestors to experience, for with Love the soul comes alive!

Animals follow a sexual impulse prompted by grace in keeping with the 'season', but they are incapable of experiencing Love as we are. God gives of His Love for our experience uniquely, but our early ancestor since 50,000 years ago needed to be taught into the ways of LOVING. Not sex as an end in itself anymore, but sex as an expression of Love. Clearly, this would be a long learning-curve for our ancestors, to be drawn into the sublime mystery of Godly sex, if I may put it that way. And clearly, a cold Ice Age would bring our family members close together at night, snuggling up intimately according to the laws of relationships. God made matters wonderfully intimate for our ancestors also by removing our bodily hair (especially that of woman) so as to make us naked and sensual to the touch. This, during an Ice age when hair would have been useful to say the least! There is indeed meaning in the madness.

Yes, men and women began to enjoy the intimacy of sex as never before, enlivened in their hearts by God's grace and Love. Love 'calls' and a man and a woman responds through their humanity. However, unbeknown to themselves, **they lacked one thing**: the loving relationship with God Himself, **He who gave them to drink of Divine Love.** [see Song of Songs 1:4 and John 4:10] Yet, more than this, God wanted to be united WITH them in their intimate communion, for ultimately, it is to this essential Reality of Divine Presence that we are truly made, to be forever blessed thereafter in His Divine Company (*just as I have testified*). Until that day, **our family remained incomplete**, but God had a plan, even before we were made He had this all planned out.

It is my belief, having gone this journey with you, and knowing that the Holy Spirit now prompted our ancestors towards this end, that there must have been **two people**, a man and a woman, who made their way into a beautiful land bordered by two rivers.

So if we follow their trail from the north, but instead of taking the coastal way towards Lebanon (along the Levantine Corridor) we in fact end up travelling between the Euphrates river to the west and the Tigris to the east, in the land of *Al Jazirah* (modern northern Iraq), and continuing southwards, we end up being shepherded into the fertile plain known as *Shinar* (modern southern Iraq) where these two great rivers converge, and where the 'tower of Babel' was built (ref. Genesis 11:2) in the land of Babylonia. In more ancient times this was the land of '**Sumer**'. It is my conviction that this particular cradle of land was the location of the 'Garden of Eden'. About 10,000 years ago when the Ice Age ended, there came into that land one man and his woman (helpmate), just as God intended.

VI. into the Garden of Eden

For 40,000 years our ancestors experienced the Ice Age, and when it ended they were mature in their humanity. We see our family making their way back from the now deserted regions in the north, looking for a new land to inhabit. And for whatever reason, from among many, a man and a woman (who loved each other) went on alone into the region of *Sumer*, brought there by God. For it was there that God determined for this man and this woman to be the first to encounter Him in all His glory, so that they would come to know and to adore the One who had created them.

Now, when the man and the woman entered the Garden of Eden, they did so in full knowledge of the world God had given His people to experience and explore over thousands of years, enjoying every stimulation, sensuous experience and pleasure of life: beauty in all its colours and forms to behold; delicacies of taste *to eat* (not just food!); textures to touch; and sounds of nature, voice and song to discover. All these wonderful aspects of experience and knowledge were theirs, but above all was the intimate and delightful knowledge of each other, enlightened by love. Thus God knew that they were now mature enough to meet their Maker; He knew that they would now have the perception enough for this profound **supernatural** encounter.

So, with this maturity and knowledge, Adam now came into the glorious Presence of his Maker, the climax of this (evolutionary) journey of **becoming truly Human**. For God made us exclusively to be Covenanted to Him. This was to be the profound Moment of Revelation, not only for the man but also for God, for by it God would unite Himself in and with a 'body of flesh' for the very first time, made and prepared for Him, and the man would experience the 'Very Presence of God' for the very first time, who is 'the True and Living Way'. (see. John 14:6; 14:17 and 14:23) Thus, what we hear recounted for us in Scripture is an historical Event that promised to change forever the human experience of life. Alas, we know that Adam did not pass <u>the test of fidelity</u> to the governing law of this God-given nature, he was not faithful to the Lord his God, but he followed Eve instead (who herself had been deceived by the serpent), and together they fell into **sin** with dire consequences.

So when we hear in the Book of Genesis the narrative about 'the man' and 'the woman' in the Garden, (ref. Genesis 2:25; 3:1–19) we should realise that this Event of Divine Intervention was to be the threshold of human perfection, the proper end to which we were made... and even now 'called'.

It is my belief that this sacred meeting place between God and Man eventually became Babylonia [the Greek form of 'Babel'], which translated means '**the Gate of God**', between the Tigris and the Euphrates rivers. You are perhaps surprised by my faith, but let us read for a moment about another 'Gate' as described by Jacob, son of Isaac, son of Abraham: "Jacob lay down to sleep and dreamt of a stairway resting on the Earth with its top reaching to Heaven, with the angels of God ascending and descending on it. When he awoke, he thought, "Surely the Lord is in this place, and I was not aware of it. How awesome is this place! This is none other than the house of God; this is **the gate of Heaven**." (ref. Genesis 28:12, 16–17) Indeed, just as 'Babel' became used and abused by man's wickedness after the Fall, so was 'Bethel' used and abused also!

But if I may divert for a moment to consider the significance of these phases, I have found some interesting details about the people of 'Sumer' whose culture predates Babylonia. Firstly, 'Sumer' literally means, 'the land of the noble Lords', or, 'the land of the Lords of Brightness' (Stiebing: 'Ancient Near Eastern History and Culture, 1994). In the ancient Sumerian manuscripts listing the kingships, the first named is 'Alulim', who was king of the city of 'Eridu' (which means 'Mighty Place'), arguably the oldest city in the world, and argued to be the original site of 'the Tower of Babel' rather than the later city of Babylon. The Sumerian list of kingships (ie: a king residing over the prevailing community/city at the time) is a long complex lineage of successive kings, but our interest is in the opening lines of this list which reads, "**After the kingship descended from heaven**, the kingship was in Eridu. In Eridu, Alulim became king." It has been suggested that 'Alulim' may be the same man as the biblical 'Adam', but my feeling is that Alulim refers to a descendent of Adam. As for Eridu, it is thought to have been founded in about 5400 BC, which is over 7,400 years ago, relatively close to my suggested 10,000. Indeed, the 'sedentary' communities upon which 'civilizations' were built in numerous localities around the world began around 10,000 years ago with what is called the Neolithic Revolution. The Sumerian culture it would seem, is the first true civilization, succeeded by others throughout the ancient Near East, which itself is considered the cradle of civilization. Thus, we can see how significant Sumer is for our theme since the original and first 'kingship' of Eridu is located but a stones throw from our Garden! But as for their system of mythic-cultural belief of 'kingships' which migrated with the seasons of inevitable political change, this is another story altogether!

So we can see how God's **grace** was at work among our ancestors all 50,000 years ago in Africa, and by grace, led them out into the Ice Age of Eurasia to explore and learn about themselves and to mature as only humans can. We can understand how and why man was in a state of innocence during these 40,000 years, but that ultimately God's plan would be to "show Himself to them". (ref. John 14:21) And that by this final Act of Fellowship and Anointing, the man and the woman would honour, praise and adore forever their Maker, submitting devotedly to His Sovereign Lordship. By this final Revelation and spiritual *inward* Knowledge, humankind would forever participate in God's very own Nature and Being, eternally grateful that they had been made. It would seem reasonable to suppose that out of many peoples God chose two individuals, a man and a woman, and drew them to a place He saw fit to TEST their fidelity to Him (and to the law of Love) through the blessed Anointing of His Very Presence. (ref. John 14:23) In this way these two persons, Adam and Eve, would have enjoyed the profound privilege of becoming the first 'children of God'.

VII. Reflecting upon 'Original Sin'

So when God revealed His Divinity to Adam, what Adam experienced was not some external apparition but in fact the supernatural **internal** Presence of the Lord of Glory. (see John

14:21–23) Adam would have experienced such blessedness, acknowledging that this spiritual Power and Majesty was not him but of God and was God, who now possessed him. He would have experienced such overwhelming elation that there could be no doubt as to its meaning. From the point of view of a creature, therefore, the supernatural 'Very Presence' (*as I have personally testified to*) demands of our honour and worship.

"You may eat of any fruit except that from the Tree of the knowledge of good and evil, for if you take and eat of it for your self satisfaction, then you will surely die." (ref. Genesis 2:17) This was the test God gave Adam, the test of faithfulness and obedience, of devotion and service, for it is by offering our most precious gifts like "the gifts of gold, of incense and of myrrh" that we show our worship of God. (see Matthew 2:11) So if we take and eat the choicest fruit for ourselves then we dishonour the One we are made to worship! And what is true worship? It is to obey the most important and first Commandment:

"Hear this, you who have fellowship with Me: the Lord your God, the Lord is One. You shall love the Lord your God with all your heart and with all your soul and with all your mind and with all your strength". (Deuteronomy 6:5; Mark 12:29–30)

It is my belief that there is only one specific action in our life that so completely fulfils and satisfies this all-consuming offering of self to another, and that is, when we **'make love'**. But let no-one tell me that the people of this *fallen* world are doing it for God! No, but for each other!! So what shall we say of our vows of undying love, service and devotion to each other? Is this right and lawful according to the truth? The straight answer is NO! For in very truth, male and female together are made to please and to serve God, thus it is with God that a man and a woman shall make their vows of love and fidelity, and it is to God that they shall devote themselves, it is to – **'God with us'** (ref. Matthew 1:23; 28:20; Titus 2:11–14) – that they shall offer their 'gold' and their 'incense' and their 'myrrh' (ref. Matthew 2:11). This is what it is to Worship and to **'make Love loved'**.

And there, in the middle of the Garden stood Adam and Eve. She had given Adam so much pleasure in the past... 'and it was good'. It was to her that he had always offered his most prized gift for her fulfilment and she her most precious gift for his satisfaction, each savouring the 'incense' of love's communing, worshipping the mystery of love found in each other. BUT NOW, God had revealed His Glorious Presence to Adam, and what was once but a Mystery now became a Divine Reality... and **<u>nothing would ever be the same again</u>**.

Consider for a moment the following: when a man sees the Image of Beauty standing before him, he will gaze in delight and bend at the knee in praise; and when a man hears a voice so sweet and pure, then his heart will thrill at hearing her voice; and when he is allowed to touch and caresses her soft velvet skin so responsive and yielding, he will be consumed with desire; and on being so close to her now, he smells the delight of her fragrance and cannot hold back any more! Her power over him is absolute, and he knows it! Such is the power a woman has over a man, and she can use it for good or for evil.

Now, I have only related the outward appearance of an inward reality, for the beauty exhibited only truly becomes desirable to LOVE when this outward beauty is the reflection of an inward purity. (ref. 1 Peter 3:3–6) Furthermore, outward attributes are gifted a person whereas what is on the inside is the true quality of a person. Yet, God Himself is the Giver of both the gifts and the qualities of His creatures. However, whereas *outward* physical attributes are unmerited, *inward* spiritual qualities of a personality are attained only through merit, since all virtue is of God and given by God as He pleases.

So what shall we say: shall a man offer himself to a woman and she him without regard for the Lord their God, or shall they offer their worship to the Lord of Glory who made both <u>for His own good pleasure</u>, notwithstanding the blessed gift of Himself to them?! Surely, the equation is simple! So, to whom shall we surrender our soul to, to whom shall we offer our heart's devotion and service to? To whom do we owe our Worship and service? Alas, the people of this world love the ways of darkness too much! (ref. John 3:19)

This, therefore, was the test given to Adam: to serve God or to gratify mere flesh. He chose to follow Eve into eating the sensual delights of love according to their earthly nature alone, (see Luke 5:39) serving this nature in each other rather than worshipping the abiding **Divinity** that Adam was now given to experience and know. This is why the greatest guilt is with Adam, not Eve! As a result, not only did God remove His

Presence from Adam but they forfeited the blessing of abiding grace that had sustained their every blessing.

For 40,000 years man's innocent heart had been fashioned and moved by God; our innocent ancestor did not know evil but lived according to the inner-governance of God's holy presence and love. But after the Fall, the *cloak* of God's abiding presence was removed and Adam and Eve realised that they were now '*naked*', and, knowing that they had done wrong, covered up their shame from God with *fig leaves*. (ref. Genesis 3:8)

This was the 'Original Sin', the transgression against holiness and truth committed by our first parents, the nature of which has everything to do with SEX! You see, by the inward revealing of the Godhead to Adam in the Garden (received as a 'birthright' since he was in a state of holy innocence), Adam would have experienced a blessed **Anointing** of God's coming upon him to take up His preordained 'Seat of Glory' in and with the man. BUT, through disobedience and pride, rather than celebrating Holy Love in adoration of their Creator who had now revealed His 'Very Presence' to them, Adam and Eve turned away from God in order to delight in themselves instead. God thus withdrew His Holy Presence from them and they lost the Inheritance of Divinity-with-them.

[Yet, according to God's redeeming grace in these days of Salvation, He has Anointed me personally with the 'Very Presence' (see John 14:23) which is why I am able to give a testimony to this Truth. (see 1John 2:20,27) However, here is not the right place for me to share with you this all-important message. You will find this unambiguous Testimony in my book, *'The Holy Covenant of Love'*].

And in like manner, each one of us must turn and be made right (again) with our Creator in order for Him to bless us and restore to us our true Humanity. For us Humans are not made to live life outside the Company of God's abiding Presence; we are not meant to be our own masters serving to satisfy ourselves! And one day soon, God will intervene again to put matters right, to bring in 'The Fulfilment', the Kingdom of God, whether we like it or not.

VIII. after the 'Fall'

So by this 'Original' disobedience and transgression, our first *parents* were barred from God's Holy Presence and even the ground upon which they stood became cursed. (ref. Genesis 3:17) And ever since this Fall, there has been enmity between a **Holy God** and a **sinful world**. So it is on account of Adam and Eve that all people have been bound over to this inordinate condition of sin, because the sanctifying Holy Spirit was taken away not just from the two in the Garden who fell, but it had to be taken away from all. For God is Holy, and the innocent world was imbued with His Spirit, but now that **sin** had entered the world, His Spirit departed in order that Man be saved and not destroyed. (see Exodus 19:20–25) And from that day on, God has been at work to overcome this curse by reconciling us back to Himself.

Even though man had forfeited the intimate company of God, he would live by obedience to the ordinances of conscience and reason, and according to the law of love in which he was made. Thus God now declares to him, "**If you do what is right, will you not be accepted by Me? But if you do not do what is right, sin is crouching at your door; it desires to have you, but you must master it**." (Genesis 4:7). Alongside this necessary response to our conscience, we all readily acknowledge the 'golden rule' of life, of, "**doing unto others as you would have them do to yourself**".

Alas, generally speaking, society has never lived by the integrity of this law and this ordinance. Instead, the story is one of endless discord and disharmony in every facet of our lives: between people and the natural world, between family relationships, communities and societies. Yes, history tells us much about the wickedness of kings and conquerors bringing violence, social injustice, oppression and slavery upon the masses; it tells us much about man's miserable subjection to these ruling cultures; and about the myriad of social crimes perpetrated amongst the masses; but it doesn't tell us much about the crimes of man's illicit sexual behaviour. Adam and Eve experienced an acute sense of shame after their illicit act, but the people of this world readily give themselves over to sin without shame! Perhaps no-where is this better illustrated than in the story of **Sodom and Gomorrah** which God was forced to finally condemn (Genesis 19:13). This is surely a grave warning to us all!

So we can see why the world that God so loved now grieved Him so much, seeing how, "every inclination of the thoughts of man's hearts was only evil all the time", that He was moved to destroy it because, "the earth was so filled with violence because of them." "But Noah found favour in the eyes of the Lord". (see Genesis 6:5–8) Yes, the sign of the Rainbow with Noah confirmed God's determination to redeem us because He loves the World that He made so much, but as soon as the doors to that Ark were opened again, again man ran off to seek his own self satisfaction as he has forever done, never more so than today! For the studies of anthropology and archaeology indicate to us a very dark picture: of war and greed, of arrogance and deceit, of vainglory and oppression, and every wickedness under the sun...! The beginning of 'civilisations', giving rise to great cities, expanding states, and conquering empires!

How ironic it is that after the Fall of Adam and the story of Cain killing his brother Abel on account of his jealousy, rivalry and resentment, we are then told by Scripture that, "at that time men began to call on the Lord God". (Genesis 4:26) Let us not forget that our **innocent** family did not know God, for God had not revealed Himself to them *personally*. It was Adam and Eve who were the first to meet with God in the Garden. This profound moment and experience would have been communicated throughout the land, which is most likely why this Place of Meeting was soon to be called **'The Gate of God'** (Babel). Clearly, such a place and such an encounter would become most famous: just imagine how such a truly amazing experience told firstly by Adam to his sons and they to their neighbours and so on, must have made an immense impact upon peoples thinking! of course "men began to call on Almighty God"! Suddenly, man has been given the ultimate notion of fellowship with a *personal* God, One who unites Himself with a mere man! Of course, fame leads to legend and its only one further thought away to endow mere men with god-like status, which is the basis of so many ancient mythologies and religions!!! For typically, after the Fall, mythologies and religions of every kind were conceived off the back of men given or attaining to stupendous power and dominion over the land, wherein common sense of right and wrong and of love are overwritten by systems of belief which are inherently corrupt, fashioned by notions ensuring a continuum of central power and said to be 'sanctioned' by the Almighty!

Indeed, Wisdom springs up only among humble men and women, who then share this inspired word, but in no time at all, what was once Wisdom for our education soon undergoes distortion to fit man's own divisive ways. It's built into the system, for the power-base nearly always falls to the ambitious and not the humble, and if not to the one, then to those who eagerly surround him!

From a political and social standpoint also, it is clear that the development of agriculture and settled farming practice was perhaps the key to man's so called 'success', for around this all important produce of the land, came the rise and fall of cities, states and empires. Clearly, the growth of agriculture allowed for the growth of larger and denser populations (with a governing Power at its centre), which of course has moulded society ever since. Kings at the top, and slaves at the bottom, all doing their bit to keep the wheels turning! Needless to say, envy, hand in hand with greed, and rank, arm in arm with prejudice, were like cement to the mortar, by which towers a mile high could be built! Such are the ways of 'the fallen', ancient and modern.

Most pertinently of all must be the name **Babel** ('Babylon' in Greek) – meaning, 'The Gate of God', which was once the Garden of Eden but which became the metaphor and epitome for wickedness in the world! (ref. Revelation 17:5) In like manner, the name given by Jacob – **Bethel** – meaning, 'The House of God', was used and abused by Jeroboam the first king of the northern kingdom of *Israel* (as opposed to the southern kingdom of *Judah*), who set up a 'golden calf' upon this sacred site simply for political control of *his* people! (see 1 Kings 12:26–30) O, what folly is done by nearly all the 'kings' of this fallen world for whom 'power' has become to them their only god!

So we hear the people say to each other in Babylon, "**Come, let us build ourselves a city, with a tower that reaches to the heavens, so that we may make a name for ourselves**..." (Genesis 11:4) In like manner, Jericho was built, in the Fertile Crescent where wheat and water came together, the envy of the world around. By a happy and Providential conjunction of natural and farming practice about 10,000 years ago, a primitive hybrid of wheat (Emmer) appeared which man has lived by ever since. This hybrid of wheat, which uniquely required farming practice for its propagation, was meant by God to be for man's mutual prosperity and wellbeing, 'calling' man away from his hunting past and introducing a 'beloved' People to grain and the making of bread instead as their staple food. Alas, 'fallen' man quickly made the best of this blessing by turning this wheat into the dominant currency of Power! This wheat grew originally around the hillsides of the Fertile Crescent and provided for ancient cities such as Jericho. But throughout Jericho's turbulent history, of envious neighbours overthrowing and replacing its inhabitants and fortifying it with ever greater defensive walls and of increasing its tower to stupendous heights, we get the message in those walls, of layer upon layer of past 'civilisations' that came, were conquered, buried, and built over time and again... so that the tower lies not so much under forty-five feet of soil as under forty-five feet of past 'civilisations'! The fact is that civilizations were never so civilised after all... of Babylonia, Egypt, and Indus, just to mention a few... just the beginning of things to come, built on the back of slaves, invasions and every exploitation under the sun... ever since Adam went it alone.

Final words

Adam and Eve were the first *called* to become 'children of God', but they went their own way and were cast out of the Garden of God's Presence. Since then, God has been at work to bring us back to Himself. But it is only in the last two thousand years that God has held His hands out wide [as on a Cross], inviting whosoever wishes to belong to Him and to enjoy the eternal inheritance that He has promised through JESUS CHRIST. How ironic it is then that in this 'fallen' world rife with falsehood and sin, so much of society today should see fit to enjoy so much prosperity to live for (while the other half lives in tears), this at a time when everything is now ready, everything is prepared, and God is about to establish the Kingdom for which we are truly meant! Through Jesus, He has done everything necessary to free us from falsehood and sin; He has in fact fully reconciled Humanity to Himself. **All He asks is for our consent, that we acknowledge His Sovereignty and reciprocate His Love**.

However, as Jesus declares, "anyone who will not receive the Kingdom of God like a little child will never enter it." (ref. Luke 18:17) Does this not remind us of those true and lowly ancestors of old. Of course, we are not 'innocent' anymore, but **a contrite and lowly heart** is of exceeding worth in God's sight and of far greater merit. It is to such as these that Jesus refers.

It is my hope and prayer that having carried out my work *best I can*, that many will hear its message and be inspired to follow the Way that leads into the Kingdom of God. You have only to fall on bended knee and to ask. (see Luke 11:13)

But whatever people may say and do, let it not be said of God that He did not reveal His Truth to us and open for us the way into the fullness of truth upon which human integrity rests. And let it not be said that I did not make it plain to you by my Testimony and by all that I have written!

For God is HOLY and made the World for His own good pleasure... and He will not give it up to SIN. Yet He has done absolutely everything possible in His merciful love to free us from sin and give us true happiness, but He will not interfere with our free will. So what do you say: Do you want to belong to your Creator and serve Him or not?

Bread became the staple diet of men, and the currency of power to boot, but as the immutable Word of God has reminded us for thousands of years, "**Man does not <u>live</u> on bread alone, but on every Word that comes from the mouth of God**". (Deut 8:1-5) When all is said and done, it was God who had the first word to say and it will be God who has the last. (ref. Revelation 22:12–13) Amen

84

Appendix

Notice to the Scientist

Helplessly I have watched on in frustration as the scientific community has pushed 'Evolution' ever further into a corner. There's nothing wrong with the research and its findings, but there is everything wrong with their assumptions! The myth of 'the selfish gene', making theories based on mere biology and fitness, like taking notes from a microscope without setting the evidence in context of the greater picture. The Big Bang theory, yes, but they blindly and quickly move on to suggest that Order can originate from chaos, despite their close observations that the entire Universe is intricately bound by profound laws of balance, order and harmony, essential to existence. Why is it that the 'scientist' will not side with Intelligence as the Divine Cause and governing principle of the universe, and realise that the origins of life itself is a mystery beyond mere particles of matter! It seems that even the mystery of Love itself must bend to this false *scientific* premise!

One reason surely is this: that to deflect their gaze from *'pure'* science would be to profess belief in God, and such thinking is frowned upon by the Scientific Community at large, as it were, compromising their authority and legitimacy in the eyes of an unbelieving world. Of course, this is not so of the entire Community nor the world, but only reflects the general consensus. There are no doubt distinguished individuals who have broken ranks, realising that Intelligence must be at work.

Then there is another reason perhaps: that Man tends to see things according to his own autonomous and solitary identity, and will fashion all existence upon this model, justifying his own self-styled existence. If only he realised the original cause of our inordinate 'self' and of our 'fall from grace' in the Garden! (ref. Genesis 3:11)

As regards Charles Darwin, the 'father' of evolutionary theory, I admire what he stood for and did, for I too would hate to the core of my being the prevailing theory of the time of *superior species*, whites over blacks!! And I too would pray to do all I could to overturn this most abhorrent mind-set and practice.

William Wilberforce did what he could with the power he held within parliament, and we are eternally grateful for his work in helping to bring an end to slavery. No less so am I grateful to Darwin for his scientific work in proving the brotherhood of man. For his *inspired* mission was to prove that mankind has a common origin, black and white. By so doing he longed to debunk the narrow and arrogant consensus of his time and bring about emancipation not just from slavery but from this grossly distorted discriminatory theory! He succeeded, and thank God for that.

Nevertheless, there must have remained for Darwin many questions left unanswered regarding his theory of 'natural selection'. Theories are not carved into stone, but ought to guide others to further knowledge. But if our minds are closed to the possibility of a Divine Cause because we refuse to believe, then we close the door on the most fundamental side of our nature, the spiritual side which makes us what we are. For since time immemorial humankind has needed and sought to lay hold of the Divine, but for all your seeking and fact-finding from the material world, your work is shackled because you have chosen to close your minds on the very idea of God. You prove this to yourselves by dissociating from those among you who choose to embrace the theory of 'Intelligent Design', for they are no longer invited to The Scientific Debate!! Is it any wonder that Science and Religion are such poles apart!

For I hold **Belief** in one hand and **Science** in the other, and am happy to find a common vision upon which to stand. But you on the other hand only hold **Science** in the one hand while refusing to look upon the other! So how can you expect to reach your goal since you are so one-sided? Indeed, there is a palpable unwillingness on the part of scientists to engage in any meaningful dialogue or exchange of views with a 'believer'.

Yes, everyone is entitled to their opinion, but 'Scientific Theory' holds of course far more responsibility than that, for it has the power to influence people's belief or disbelief; it has the power to enlighten or to cast its shadow.

It is my hope then that this small book I have written may go some way to answering the unwritten questions that perplexed all those scientists of old who had both hands open in prayer. Alas, I don't suppose it will have much influence to bear upon the *'matter'* you so strongly believe in.

ACKNOWLEDGMENTS

1. I wish to give special thanks to Jean M. Auel for her 'Earth's Children' series of novels which made a marked impression upon me and led me to wonder about our ancestors in such a creative and real way.

2. "The Human Past: World Prehistory & the Development of Human Society", edited by Chris Scarre, Thames & Hudson 2005.

NOTICE TO THE READER

This book was written on completion of my principle Testimony, entitled, *The Holy Covenant of Love* for which I have set up a Website. You will find introductions to both books and a series of short essays for further reading and explanation to the themes relevant to my Testimony. In addition, you will find Links to facilitate purchase of these two books.

My Website address is: www.mysteryofourlife.com